THIS IS A CARLTON BOOK

This edition published by Carlton Books Limited 1995

ISBN 1 85868 097 2

Printed and bound in Italy.

Designed and Typeset by Archetype Ltd.

3D Stereograms were created in Mystify 3D courtesy of Oliver Fuhrer

The hidden dimension

"More than meets the eye," is what this book is about.

We all like puzzles: they tax the brain and entertain the mind with their solutions. The recent success of stereograms like the ones in this book proves that we never tire of puzzles, whatever form they take—in this case visual. Not only are stereograms beautiful pages to look at, they also turn a flat piece of paper into a three-dimensional treasure trove only your eyes can unlock. Like any treasure, seeking it can become addictive. So beware: once you've grasped one stereogram, the lure of the tantalising patterns becomes irresistible—to the point where people have been known to begin intensely staring at wallpaper or the carpet beneath their feet, just in case they missed a nugget of golden 3D!

Most of you will know how to penetrate to the hidden image floating in 3D beneath the pattern on the page, but for the newcomers here are some short tips to get to stereogram reality: In a quiet, well-lit place, sit and hold up the page level with and quite close to your eyes. Now focus as if you are looking at something much further away than the book you are holding. Relax and take in the out-of-focus pattern before you. Slowly move the page away from you, and soon the blurred pattern turns into multi-layered shapes which form the hidden image. Once you have caught a part of it, concentrate and let your eyes roam over the whole 3D object to enjoy all the details. Gently altering the angle of the book this way and that adds to the reality of the solid image.

These three images are the solutions to the stereograms featured on the cover and the previous pages.
The solutions to all other stereograms are in the reference section on page 36.

As with all things practice makes perfect, and having successfully found and enjoyed a few hidden images you'll discover you can, with little effort, see them even at a distance, in a crowded bookshop or through a window. So don't miss out. If you have trouble seeing the images, ask a friend who knows how to help you. Persevere and you will find the treasure.

Stereograms are fun!

We won't bore you with the intricacies of the technology required to create the images, nor the scientific reasons why you can see them at all. You've got the book because you want to have fun, and that is what we've aimed for.

You are about to enjoy action, jokes and… the odd monster, here and there: a whole alternate reality to take you out of your day-to-day world, and which you can dip into again and again whenever you feel like it. The patterns interrelate with the hidden images. Often they give a clue to what you will discover, sometimes they form an amusing contrast and a few times they become part of the 3D picture itself.

We hope you have as much fun with this book as we did producing the stereograms and patterns. And if you really go 3D blind, we've been kind: check out the last page for the lazy person's guide to the magical mystery tour!

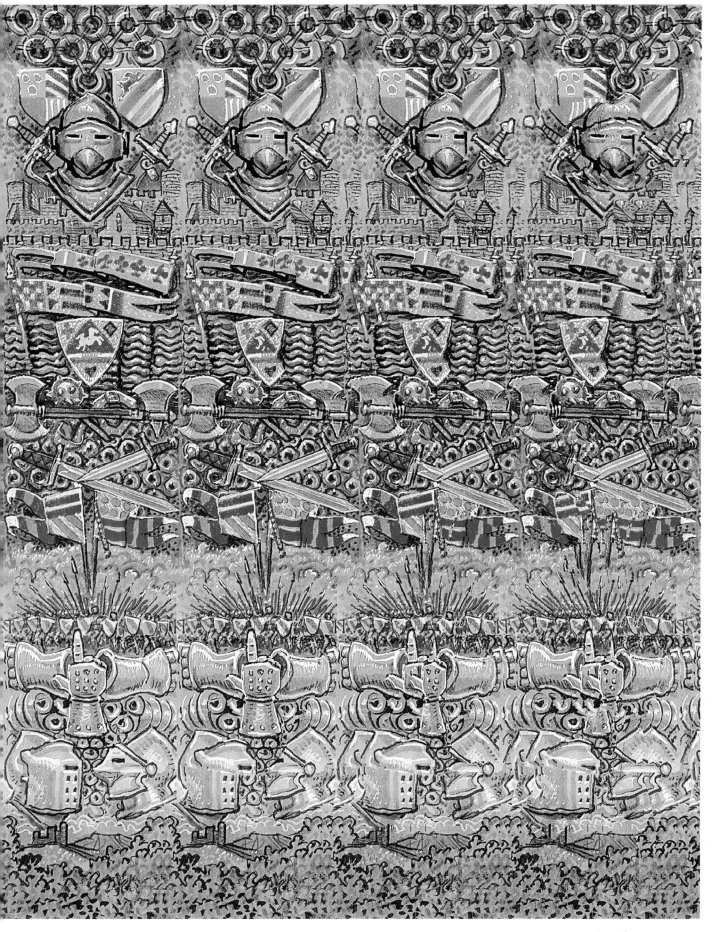

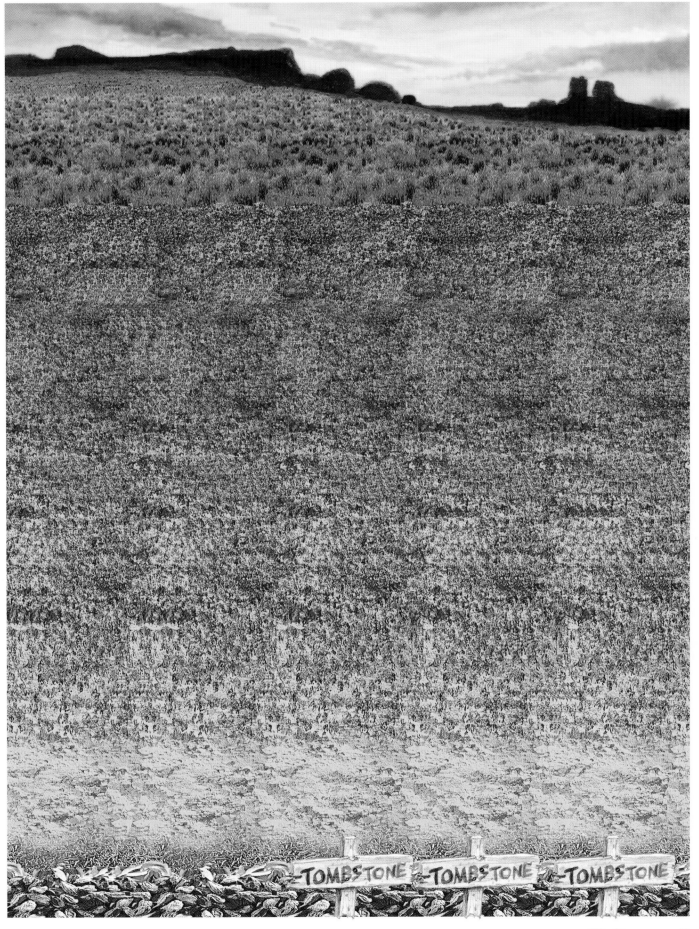

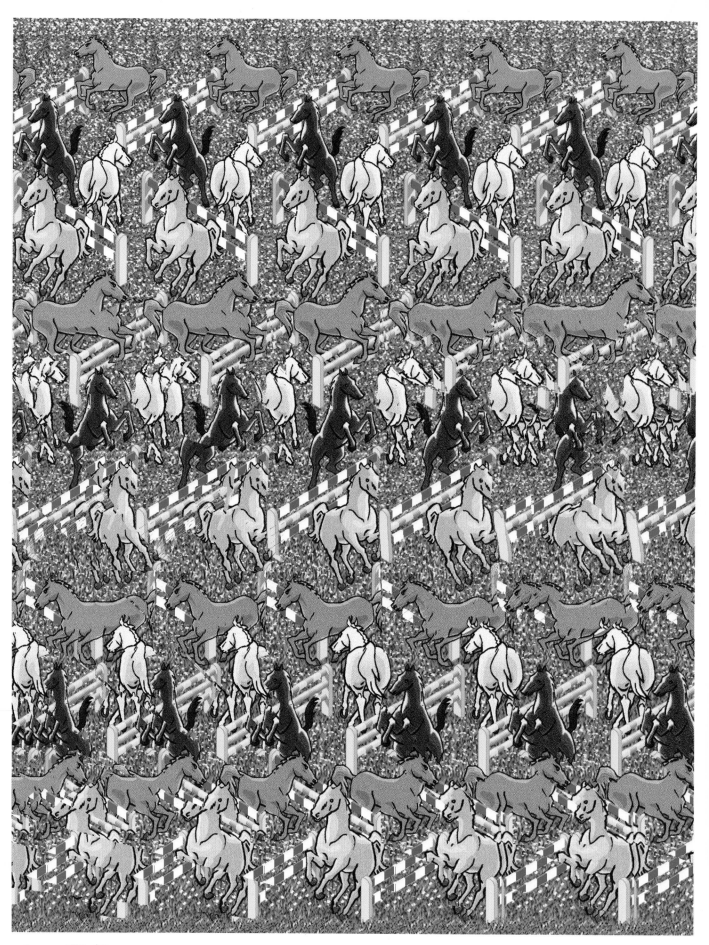

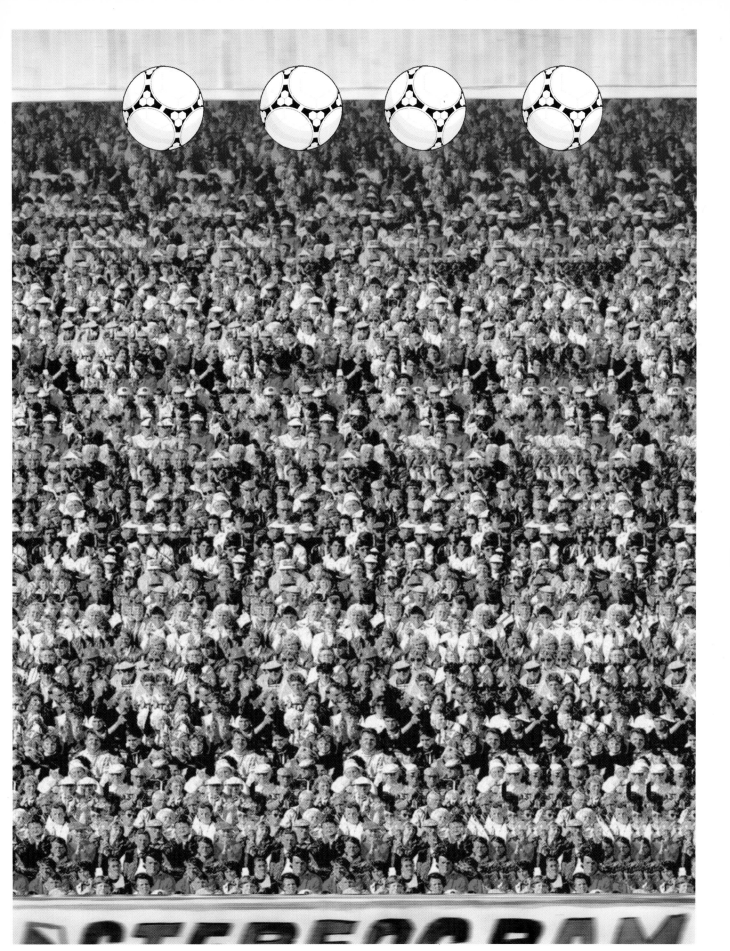

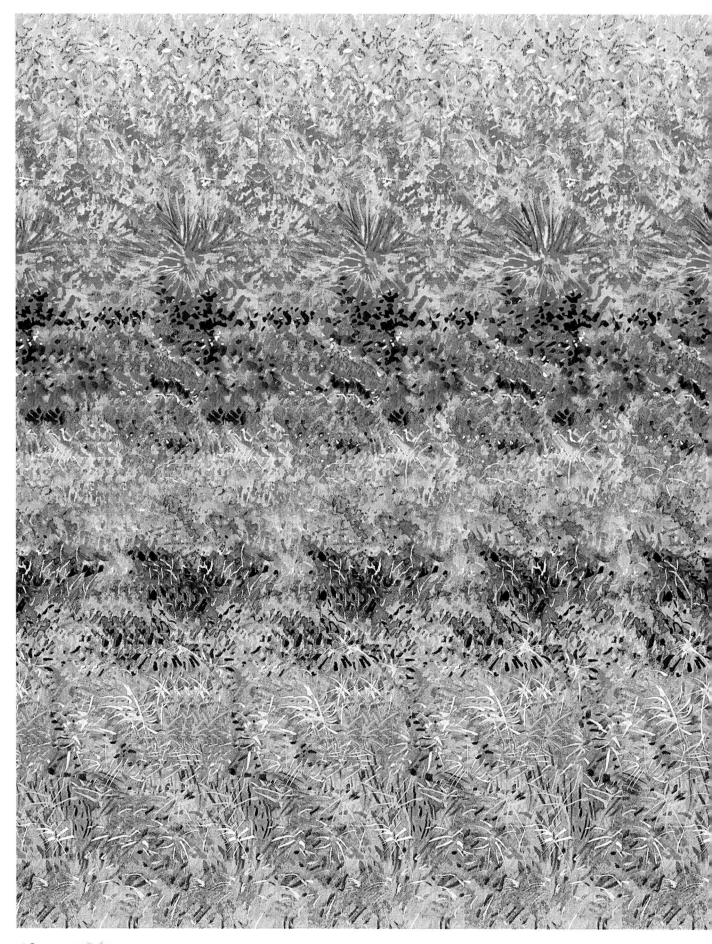

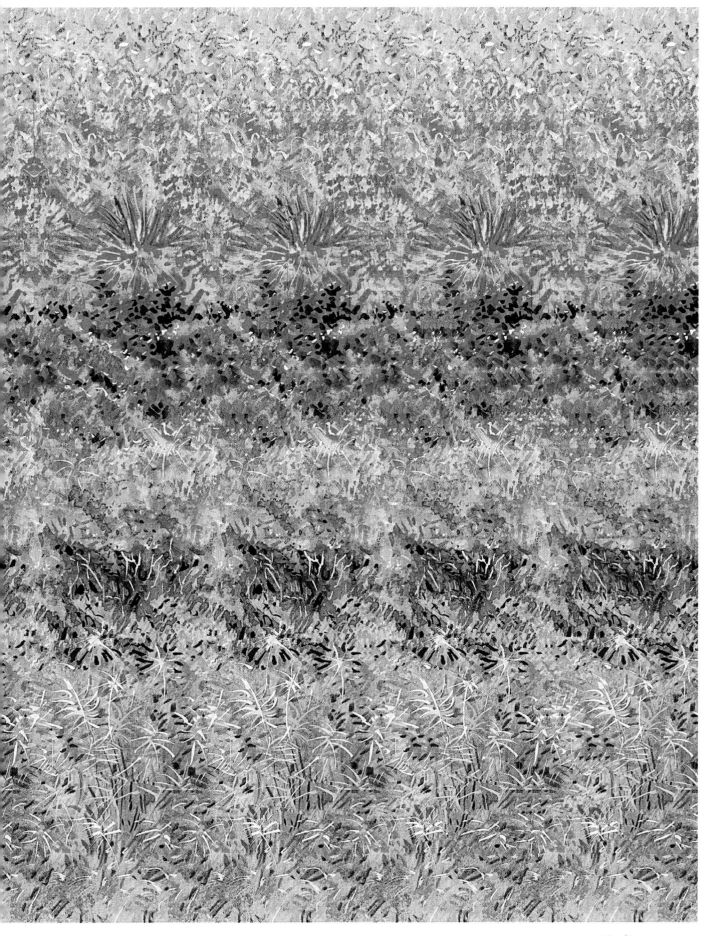

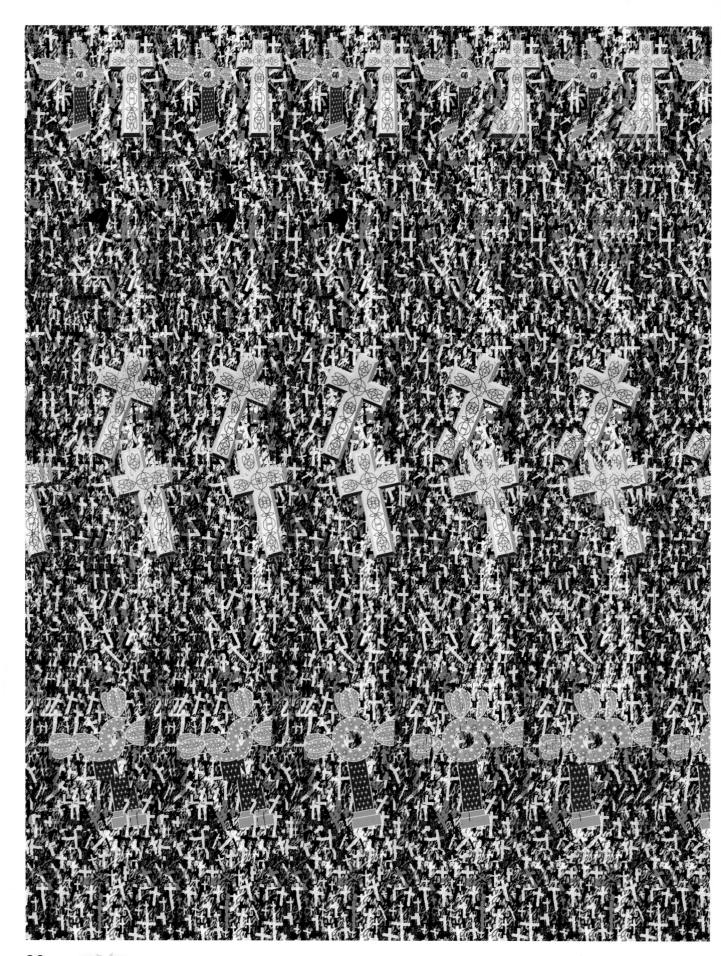

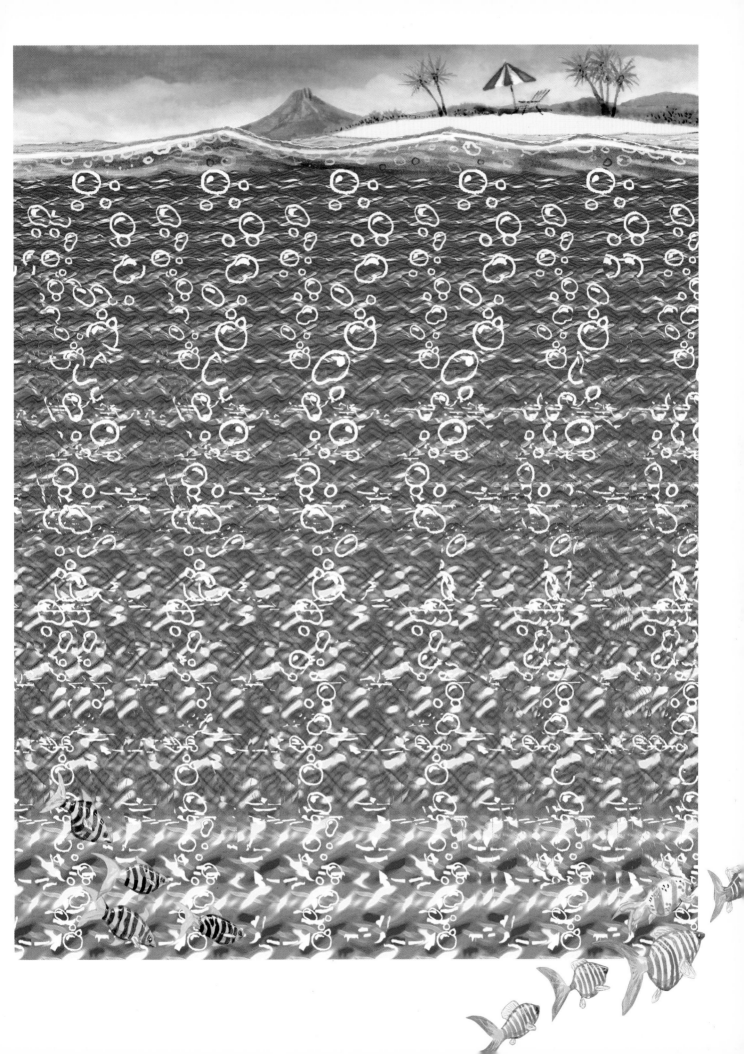

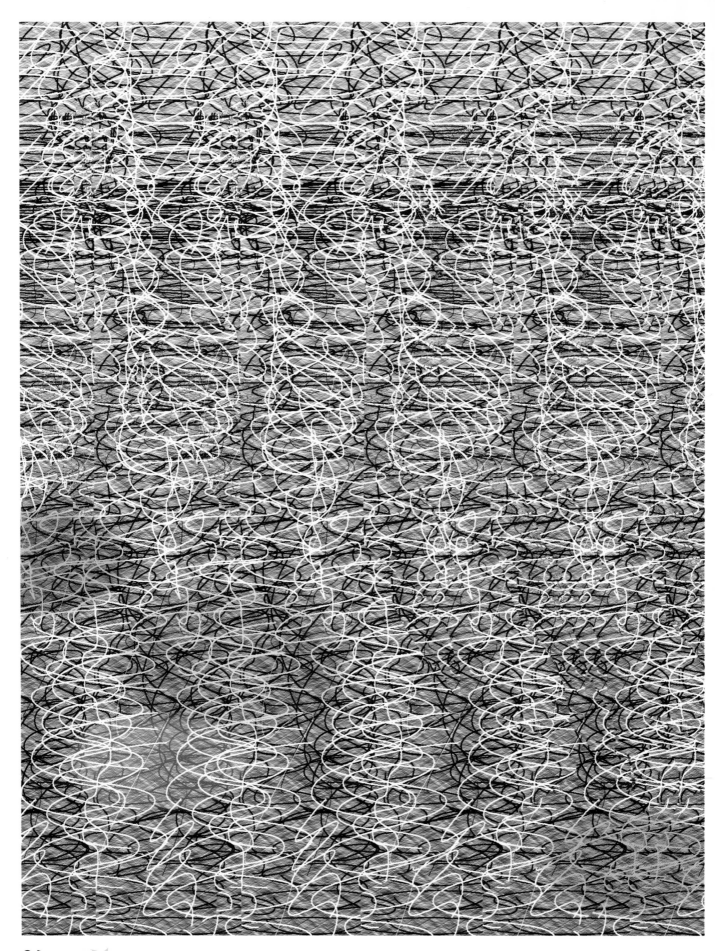

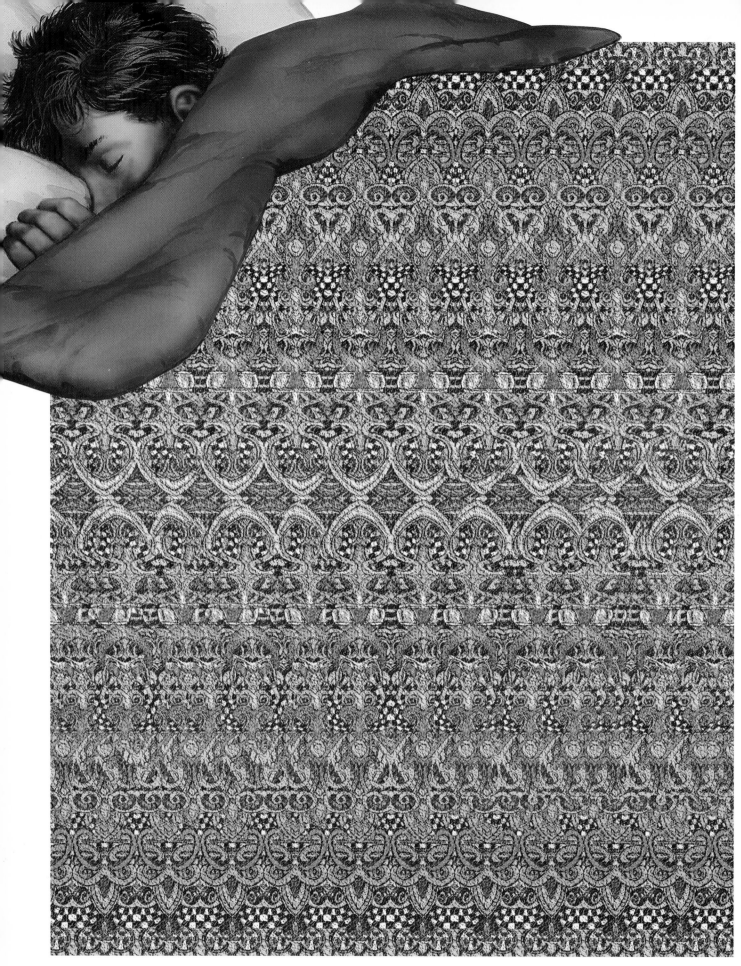

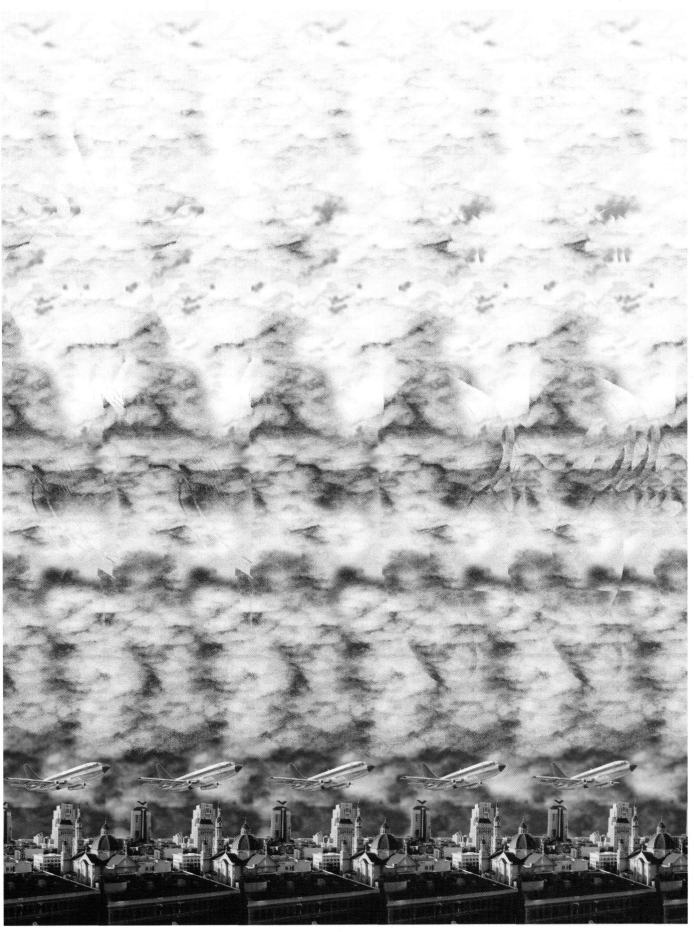

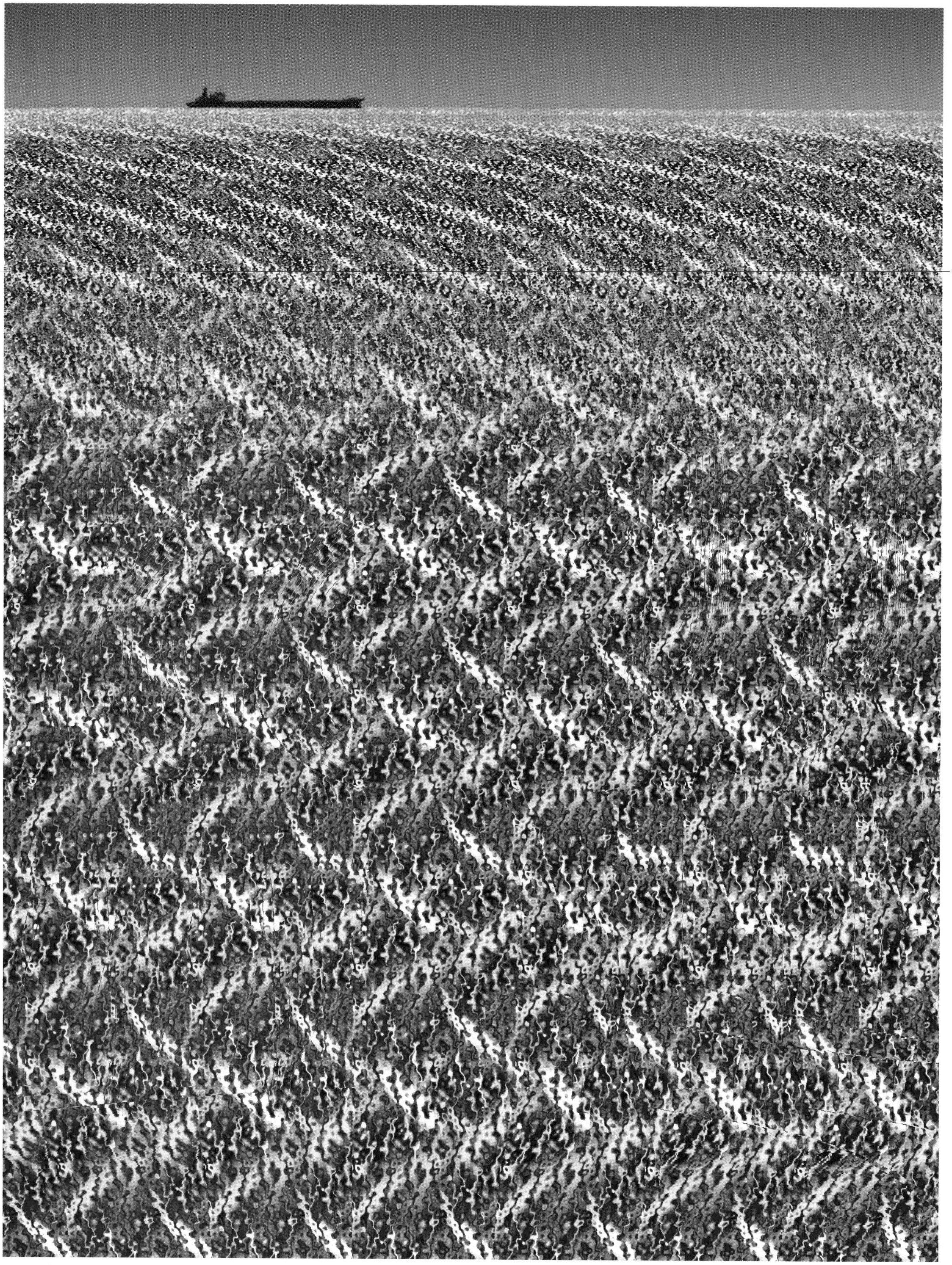

Pages 6-7

Page 8

Page 9

Page 10

Page 11

Page 12

Page 13

Page 14

Page 15

Page 16

Page 17

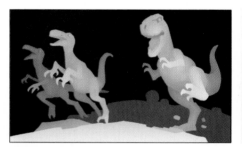
Pages 18-19

Page 20

Page 21

Page 22

Page 23

Page 24

Page 25

Page 26

Page 27

Page 28

Page 29

Pages 30-31

Page 32

Page 33

Page 34

Page 35

36